Blank Cookbook

Recipes & Notes

William Boston

Recipe Name: *Page #*

_____   _____

_____   _____

_____   _____

_____   _____

_____   _____

_____   _____

_____   _____

_____   _____

_____   _____

_____   _____

_____   _____

_____   _____

_____   _____

_____   _____

_____   _____

_____   _____

_____   _____

_____   _____

Recipe Name: *Page #*

Recipe Name:	Page #

Recipe Name: *Page #*

_____   _____

_____   _____

_____   _____

_____   _____

_____   _____

_____   _____

_____   _____

_____   _____

_____   _____

_____   _____

_____   _____

_____   _____

_____   _____

_____   _____

_____   _____

_____   _____

_____   _____

_____   _____

Recipe Name: *Page #*

_____   _____

_____   _____

_____   _____

_____   _____

_____   _____

_____   _____

_____   _____

_____   _____

_____   _____

_____   _____

_____   _____

_____   _____

_____   _____

_____   _____

_____   _____

_____   _____

_____   _____

_____   _____

_____   _____

_____   _____

Recipe Name:

Page #

_____   _____

_____   _____

_____   _____

_____   _____

_____   _____

_____   _____

_____   _____

_____   _____

_____   _____

_____   _____

_____   _____

_____   _____

_____   _____

_____   _____

_____   _____

_____   _____

_____   _____

Recipe Name: _____

Prep Time: _____ *Cook Time*: _____ *Serves*: _____

Ingredients

_____

_____

_____

_____

_____

_____

_____

_____

_____

_____

_____

_____

_____

_____

Directions

_____

_____

_____

_____

_____

_____

_____

_____

_____

_____

_____

_____

_____

Note: _____

_____

_____

_____

Page no.

Recipe Name: _____

Prep Time: _____ *Cook Time:* _____ *Serves:* _____

Ingredients   Directions

Note: _____

_____

_____

_____

Recipe Name: _____

Prep Time: _____*Cook Time:* _____ *Serves:* _____

Ingredients   *Directions*

_____ _____
_____ _____
_____ _____
_____ _____
_____ _____
_____ _____
_____ _____
_____ _____
_____ _____
_____ _____
_____ _____
_____ _____
_____ _____

Note: _____
_____
_____
_____

Page no.

Recipe Name: _____

Prep Time: _____ *Cook Time:* _____ *Serves:* _____

Ingredients

Directions

_____

_____

_____

_____

_____

_____

_____

_____

_____

_____

_____

_____

_____

_____

Note: _____

_____

_____

_____

Page no.

Recipe Name: _____

Prep Time: _____ *Cook Time:* _____ *Serves:* _____

Ingredients   ## Directions

_____   _____

_____   _____

_____   _____

_____   _____

_____   _____

_____   _____

_____   _____

_____   _____

_____   _____

_____   _____

_____   _____

_____   _____

Note: _____

_____

_____

_____

Page no.

Recipe Name: _____

Prep Time: _____ *Cook Time:* _____ *Serves:* _____

Ingredients

Directions

_____

_____

_____

_____

_____

_____

_____

_____

_____

_____

_____

_____

_____

_____

_____

Note: _____

_____

_____

_____

Page no.

Recipe Name*: _____*

Prep Time: _____Cook Time: _____ Serves: _____

Ingredients   ## Directions

_____   _____
_____   _____
_____   _____
_____   _____
_____   _____
_____   _____
_____   _____
_____   _____
_____   _____
_____   _____
_____   _____
_____   _____
_____   _____
_____   _____

Note: _____
_____
_____
_____

Page no.

Recipe Name: _____

Prep Time: _____ *Cook Time:* _____ *Serves:* _____

Ingredients   ## *Directions*

_____   _____
_____   _____
_____   _____
_____   _____
_____   _____
_____   _____
_____   _____
_____   _____
_____   _____
_____   _____
_____   _____
_____   _____
_____   _____
_____   _____
_____   _____

Note: _____

_____

_____

_____

Page no.

Recipe Name: _____

Prep Time: _____ *Cook Time:* _____ *Serves:* _____

Ingredients   ## Directions

_____   _____
_____   _____
_____   _____
_____   _____
_____   _____
_____   _____
_____   _____
_____   _____
_____   _____
_____   _____
_____   _____
_____   _____
_____   _____
_____   _____
_____   _____
_____   _____

Note: _____
_____
_____
_____

Page no.

Recipe Name: _____

Prep Time: _____ *Cook Time:* _____ *Serves:* _____

Ingredients   ## Directions

_____   _____

_____   _____

_____   _____

_____   _____

_____   _____

_____   _____

_____   _____

_____   _____

_____   _____

_____   _____

_____   _____

_____   _____

_____   _____

_____   _____

_____   _____

Note: _____

_____

_____

_____

Page no.

Recipe Name: _____

Prep Time: _____ *Cook Time:* _____ *Serves:* _____

Ingredients   ## *Directions*

_____   _____

_____   _____

_____   _____

_____   _____

_____   _____

_____   _____

_____   _____

_____   _____

_____   _____

_____   _____

_____   _____

_____   _____

_____   _____

_____   _____

Note: _____

_____

_____

_____

Page no.

Recipe Name: _____

Prep Time: _____ *Cook Time:* _____ *Serves:* _____

Ingredients   ## *Directions*

_____   _____

_____   _____

_____   _____

_____   _____

_____   _____

_____   _____

_____   _____

_____   _____

_____   _____

_____   _____

_____   _____

_____   _____

_____   _____

_____   _____

_____   _____

Note: _____

_____

_____

_____

Page no.

Recipe Name: _____

Prep Time: _____ *Cook Time:* _____ *Serves:* _____

Ingredients   ## Directions

_____   _____

_____   _____

_____   _____

_____   _____

_____   _____

_____   _____

_____   _____

_____   _____

_____   _____

_____   _____

_____   _____

_____   _____

Note: _____

_____

_____

_____

Page no.

Recipe Name: _____

Prep Time: _____ *Cook Time:* _____ *Serves:* _____

Ingredients   ## Directions

_____   _____

_____   _____

_____   _____

_____   _____

_____   _____

_____   _____

_____   _____

_____   _____

_____   _____

_____   _____

_____   _____

_____   _____

_____   _____

_____   _____

_____   _____

Note: _____

_____

_____

_____

Page no.

Recipe Name*: _____*

Prep Time: _____Cook Time: _____ Serves: _____

Ingredients   ## *Directions*

Ingredients	Directions
_____	_____
_____	_____
_____	_____
_____	_____
_____	_____
_____	_____
_____	_____
_____	_____
_____	_____
_____	_____
_____	_____
_____	_____
_____	_____

Note: _____

_____

_____

_____

Recipe Name: _____

Prep Time: _____ *Cook Time:* _____ *Serves:* _____

Ingredients

Directions

_____
_____
_____
_____
_____
_____
_____
_____
_____
_____
_____
_____
_____
_____
_____
_____

Note: _____
_____
_____
_____

Page no.

Recipe Name: _____

Prep Time: _____ *Cook Time:* _____ *Serves:* _____

Ingredients   ## Directions

_____   _____
_____   _____
_____   _____
_____   _____
_____   _____
_____   _____
_____   _____
_____   _____
_____   _____
_____   _____
_____   _____
_____   _____
_____   _____
_____   _____
_____   _____

Note: _____
_____
_____
_____

Page no.

Recipe Name: _____

Prep Time: _____ *Cook Time:* _____ *Serves:* _____

Ingredients   Directions

_____ | _____
_____ | _____
_____ | _____
_____ | _____
_____ | _____
_____ | _____
_____ | _____
_____ | _____
_____ | _____
_____ | _____
_____ | _____
_____ | _____
_____ | _____
_____ | _____

Note: _____

_____

_____

_____

Page no.

Recipe Name: _____

Prep Time: _____ *Cook Time:* _____ *Serves:* _____

Ingredients   ## Directions

_____   _____
_____   _____
_____   _____
_____   _____
_____   _____
_____   _____
_____   _____
_____   _____
_____   _____
_____   _____
_____   _____
_____   _____
_____   _____

Note: _____
_____
_____
_____

Page no.

Recipe Name: _____

Prep Time: _____ *Cook Time:* _____ *Serves:* _____

Ingredients   ## Directions

_____   _____

_____   _____

_____   _____

_____   _____

_____   _____

_____   _____

_____   _____

_____   _____

_____   _____

_____   _____

_____   _____

_____   _____

_____   _____

Note: _____

_____

_____

_____

| Page no. |

Recipe Name: _____

Prep Time: _____ *Cook Time:* _____ *Serves:* _____

Ingredients   ## Directions

_____   _____
_____   _____
_____   _____
_____   _____
_____   _____
_____   _____
_____   _____
_____   _____
_____   _____
_____   _____
_____   _____
_____   _____
_____   _____
_____   _____

Note: _____
_____
_____
_____

Page no.

Recipe Name: _____

Prep Time: _____ *Cook Time:* _____ *Serves:* _____

Ingredients

Directions

_____

_____

_____

_____

_____

_____

_____

_____

_____

_____

_____

_____

_____

_____

_____

_____

Note: _____

_____

_____

_____

Page no.

Recipe Name: _____

Prep Time: _____ *Cook Time:* _____ *Serves:* _____

Ingredients   ## Directions

_____ | _____
_____ | _____
_____ | _____
_____ | _____
_____ | _____
_____ | _____
_____ | _____
_____ | _____
_____ | _____
_____ | _____
_____ | _____
_____ | _____
_____ | _____
_____ | _____

Note: _____
_____
_____
_____

Page no.

Recipe Name: _____

Prep Time: _____ *Cook Time:* _____ *Serves:* _____

Ingredients   ## Directions

_____   _____

_____   _____

_____   _____

_____   _____

_____   _____

_____   _____

_____   _____

_____   _____

_____   _____

_____   _____

_____   _____

_____   _____

_____   _____

_____   _____

_____   _____

Note: _____

_____

_____

_____

Page no.

Recipe Name: _____

Prep Time: _____ *Cook Time:* _____ *Serves:* _____

Ingredients   ## Directions

_____

_____   _____

_____   _____

_____   _____

_____   _____

_____   _____

_____   _____

_____   _____

_____   _____

_____   _____

_____   _____

_____   _____

_____   _____

_____   _____

_____   _____

Note: _____

_____

_____

_____

Page no.

Recipe Name: _____

Prep Time: _____ *Cook Time:* _____ *Serves:* _____

Ingredients

Directions

_____

_____

_____

_____

_____

_____

_____

_____

_____

_____

_____

_____

_____

_____

Note: _____

_____

_____

_____

Recipe Name: _____

Prep Time: _____ *Cook Time:* _____ *Serves:* _____

Ingredients   ## Directions

_____ | _____
_____ | _____
_____ | _____
_____ | _____
_____ | _____
_____ | _____
_____ | _____
_____ | _____
_____ | _____
_____ | _____
_____ | _____
_____ | _____
_____ | _____
_____ | _____

Note: _____
_____
_____
_____

Page no.

Recipe Name: _____

Prep Time: _____ *Cook Time:* _____ *Serves:* _____

Ingredients

Directions

_____
_____
_____
_____
_____
_____
_____
_____
_____
_____
_____
_____
_____
_____
_____

Note: _____

_____
_____
_____

Page no.

Recipe Name: _____

Prep Time: _____ *Cook Time:* _____ *Serves:* _____

Ingredients   ## Directions

_____ | _____

_____ | _____

_____ | _____

_____ | _____

_____ | _____

_____ | _____

_____ | _____

_____ | _____

_____ | _____

_____ | _____

_____ | _____

_____ | _____

_____ | _____

_____ | _____

_____ | _____

Note: _____

_____

_____

_____

Page no.

Recipe Name: _____

Prep Time: _____ *Cook Time:* _____ *Serves:* _____

Ingredients   Directions

_____   _____
_____   _____
_____   _____
_____   _____
_____   _____
_____   _____
_____   _____
_____   _____
_____   _____
_____   _____
_____   _____
_____   _____
_____   _____
_____   _____

Note: _____

_____

_____

_____

Page no.

Recipe Name: _____

Prep Time: _____ *Cook Time:* _____ *Serves:* _____

Ingredients	*Directions*
_____	_____
_____	_____
_____	_____
_____	_____
_____	_____
_____	_____
_____	_____
_____	_____
_____	_____
_____	_____
_____	_____
_____	_____
_____	_____
_____	_____

Note: _____

_____

_____

_____

Page no.

Recipe Name: _____

Prep Time: _____ *Cook Time:* _____ *Serves:* _____

Ingredients   Directions

Ingredients	Directions
_____	_____
_____	_____
_____	_____
_____	_____
_____	_____
_____	_____
_____	_____
_____	_____
_____	_____
_____	_____
_____	_____
_____	_____
_____	_____
_____	_____
_____	_____

Note: _____

_____

_____

_____

Page no.

Recipe Name: _____

Prep Time: _____ *Cook Time:* _____ *Serves:* _____

Ingredients	*Directions*
_____	_____
_____	_____
_____	_____
_____	_____
_____	_____
_____	_____
_____	_____
_____	_____
_____	_____
_____	_____
_____	_____
_____	_____
_____	_____
_____	_____

Note: _____

_____

_____

_____

Page no.

Recipe Name*: _____*
Prep Time: _____Cook Time: _____ Serves: _____

Ingredients   ## Directions

_____   _____
_____   _____
_____   _____
_____   _____
_____   _____
_____   _____
_____   _____
_____   _____
_____   _____
_____   _____
_____   _____
_____   _____
_____   _____
_____   _____

Note: _____
_____
_____
_____

Page no.

Recipe Name: _____

Prep Time: _____ *Cook Time:* _____ *Serves:* _____

Ingredients	**Directions**
_____	_____
_____	_____
_____	_____
_____	_____
_____	_____
_____	_____
_____	_____
_____	_____
_____	_____
_____	_____
_____	_____
_____	_____
_____	_____

Note: _____

_____

_____

_____

Page no.

Recipe Name: _____

Prep Time: _____ *Cook Time:* _____ *Serves:* _____

Ingredients   ## Directions

_____ | _____
_____ | _____
_____ | _____
_____ | _____
_____ | _____
_____ | _____
_____ | _____
_____ | _____
_____ | _____
_____ | _____
_____ | _____
_____ | _____
_____ | _____
_____ | _____

Note: _____

_____

_____

_____

Recipe Name: _____

Prep Time: _____ *Cook Time:* _____ *Serves:* _____

Ingredients   ## *Directions*

_____   _____
_____   _____
_____   _____
_____   _____
_____   _____
_____   _____
_____   _____
_____   _____
_____   _____
_____   _____
_____   _____
_____   _____
_____   _____
_____   _____
_____   _____
_____   _____

Note: _____

_____

_____

_____

Page no.

Recipe Name: _____

Prep Time: _____ *Cook Time:* _____ *Serves:* _____

Ingredients   ## Directions

_____   _____
_____   _____
_____   _____
_____   _____
_____   _____
_____   _____
_____   _____
_____   _____
_____   _____
_____   _____
_____   _____
_____   _____
_____   _____
_____   _____

Note: _____

_____

_____

_____

Page no.

Recipe Name: _____

Prep Time: _____ *Cook Time:* _____ *Serves:* _____

Ingredients   Directions

Ingredients	Directions
_____	_____
_____	_____
_____	_____
_____	_____
_____	_____
_____	_____
_____	_____
_____	_____
_____	_____
_____	_____
_____	_____
_____	_____
_____	_____
_____	_____

Note: _____
_____
_____
_____

Page no.

Recipe Name: _____

Prep Time: _____ *Cook Time:* _____ *Serves:* _____

Ingredients

Directions

Note: _____

_____

_____

_____

Page no.

Recipe Name: _____

Prep Time: _____ *Cook Time:* _____ *Serves:* _____

Ingredients   *Directions*

_____ | _____
_____ | _____
_____ | _____
_____ | _____
_____ | _____
_____ | _____
_____ | _____
_____ | _____
_____ | _____
_____ | _____
_____ | _____
_____ | _____
_____ | _____
_____ | _____

Note: _____

_____

_____

_____

Page no.

Recipe Name: _____

Prep Time: _____ *Cook Time:* _____ *Serves:* _____

Ingredients

Directions

_____

_____

_____

_____

_____

_____

_____

_____

_____

_____

_____

_____

_____

_____

Note: _____

_____

_____

_____

Page no.

Recipe Name: _____

Prep Time: _____ Cook Time: _____ Serves: _____

Ingredients   ## Directions

_____   _____
_____   _____
_____   _____
_____   _____
_____   _____
_____   _____
_____   _____
_____   _____
_____   _____
_____   _____
_____   _____
_____   _____
_____   _____
_____   _____

Note: _____

_____

_____

_____

Page no.

Recipe Name: _____

Prep Time: _____ *Cook Time:* _____ *Serves:* _____

Ingredients   ## Directions

_____ | _____
_____ | _____
_____ | _____
_____ | _____
_____ | _____
_____ | _____
_____ | _____
_____ | _____
_____ | _____
_____ | _____
_____ | _____
_____ | _____
_____ | _____
_____ | _____
_____ | _____

Note: _____

_____

_____

_____

Page no.

Recipe Name: _____

Prep Time: _____ *Cook Time:* _____ *Serves:* _____

Ingredients   Directions

_____   _____
_____   _____
_____   _____
_____   _____
_____   _____
_____   _____
_____   _____
_____   _____
_____   _____
_____   _____
_____   _____
_____   _____
_____   _____
_____   _____

Note: _____

_____

_____

_____

| Page no. |

Recipe Name: _____

Prep Time: _____*Cook Time:* _____ *Serves:* _____

Ingredients   ## Directions

_____   _____
_____   _____
_____   _____
_____   _____
_____   _____
_____   _____
_____   _____
_____   _____
_____   _____
_____   _____
_____   _____
_____   _____
_____   _____
_____   _____
_____   _____
_____   _____

Note: _____

_____

_____

_____

| Page no. |

Recipe Name: _____

Prep Time: _____*Cook Time*: _____ *Serves*: _____

Ingredients   ## Directions

_____ | _____

_____ | _____

_____ | _____

_____ | _____

_____ | _____

_____ | _____

_____ | _____

_____ | _____

_____ | _____

_____ | _____

_____ | _____

_____ | _____

_____ | _____

Note: _____

_____

_____

_____

Page no.

Recipe Name: _____

Prep Time: _____ *Cook Time:* _____ *Serves:* _____

Ingredients   ## Directions

_____ | _____
_____ | _____
_____ | _____
_____ | _____
_____ | _____
_____ | _____
_____ | _____
_____ | _____
_____ | _____
_____ | _____
_____ | _____
_____ | _____
_____ | _____
_____ | _____

Note: _____

_____

_____

_____

Page no.

Recipe Name: _____

Prep Time: _____ *Cook Time:* _____ *Serves:* _____

Ingredients   ## *Directions*

_____   _____

_____   _____

_____   _____

_____   _____

_____   _____

_____   _____

_____   _____

_____   _____

_____   _____

_____   _____

_____   _____

_____   _____

_____   _____

_____   _____

Note: _____

_____

_____

_____

Page no.

Recipe Name: _____

Prep Time: _____ *Cook Time:* _____ *Serves:* _____

Ingredients   ### Directions

_____   _____
_____   _____
_____   _____
_____   _____
_____   _____
_____   _____
_____   _____
_____   _____
_____   _____
_____   _____
_____   _____
_____   _____
_____   _____
_____   _____

Note: _____
_____
_____
_____

Page no.

Recipe Name: _____

Prep Time: _____ *Cook Time:* _____ *Serves:* _____

Ingredients   ## Directions

_____   _____

_____   _____

_____   _____

_____   _____

_____   _____

_____   _____

_____   _____

_____   _____

_____   _____

_____   _____

_____   _____

_____   _____

_____   _____

_____   _____

Note: _____

_____

_____

_____

Page no.

Recipe Name: _____

Prep Time: _____ *Cook Time:* _____ *Serves:* _____

Ingredients

Directions

_____
_____
_____
_____
_____
_____
_____
_____
_____
_____
_____
_____
_____
_____

Note: _____
_____
_____
_____

Page no.

Recipe Name: _____

Prep Time: _____ *Cook Time:* _____ *Serves:* _____

Ingredients	*Directions*
_____	_____
_____	_____
_____	_____
_____	_____
_____	_____
_____	_____
_____	_____
_____	_____
_____	_____
_____	_____
_____	_____
_____	_____
_____	_____
_____	_____

Note: _____

_____

_____

_____

Recipe Name: _____

Prep Time: _____ *Cook Time:* _____ *Serves:* _____

Ingredients   ## Directions

_____   _____
_____   _____
_____   _____
_____   _____
_____   _____
_____   _____
_____   _____
_____   _____
_____   _____
_____   _____
_____   _____
_____   _____
_____   _____
_____   _____
_____   _____

Note: _____
_____
_____
_____

Page no.

Recipe Name: _____

Prep Time: _____ *Cook Time:* _____ *Serves:* _____

Ingredients	Directions
_____	_____
_____	_____
_____	_____
_____	_____
_____	_____
_____	_____
_____	_____
_____	_____
_____	_____
_____	_____
_____	_____
_____	_____
_____	_____
_____	_____

Note: _____

_____

_____

_____

| Page no. |

Recipe Name: _____

Prep Time: _____ *Cook Time:* _____ *Serves:* _____

Ingredients   ## Directions

_____   _____
_____   _____
_____   _____
_____   _____
_____   _____
_____   _____
_____   _____
_____   _____
_____   _____
_____   _____
_____   _____
_____   _____
_____   _____
_____   _____
_____   _____

Note: _____

_____
_____
_____

Page no.

Recipe Name: _____

Prep Time: _____ *Cook Time:* _____ *Serves:* _____

Ingredients   Directions

_____   _____
_____   _____
_____   _____
_____   _____
_____   _____
_____   _____
_____   _____
_____   _____
_____   _____
_____   _____
_____   _____
_____   _____
_____   _____
_____   _____
_____   _____

Note: _____

_____

_____

_____

Page no.

Recipe Name: _____

Prep Time: _____ *Cook Time:* _____ *Serves:* _____

Ingredients   ## Directions

_____   _____
_____   _____
_____   _____
_____   _____
_____   _____
_____   _____
_____   _____
_____   _____
_____   _____
_____   _____
_____   _____
_____   _____
_____   _____
_____   _____

Note: _____

_____

_____

_____

Page no.

Recipe Name: _____

Prep Time: _____*Cook Time:* _____ *Serves:* _____

Ingredients	**Directions**
_____	_____
_____	_____
_____	_____
_____	_____
_____	_____
_____	_____
_____	_____
_____	_____
_____	_____
_____	_____
_____	_____
_____	_____
_____	_____
_____	_____

Note: _____

_____

_____

_____

Page no.

Recipe Name: _____

Prep Time: _____ *Cook Time:* _____ *Serves:* _____

Ingredients   ## Directions

_____   _____
_____   _____
_____   _____
_____   _____
_____   _____
_____   _____
_____   _____
_____   _____
_____   _____
_____   _____
_____   _____
_____   _____
_____   _____
_____   _____
_____   _____
_____   _____

Note: _____

_____

_____

_____

Page no.

Recipe Name*: _____*

Prep Time: _____ Cook Time: _____ Serves: _____

Ingredients	*Directions*
_____	_____
_____	_____
_____	_____
_____	_____
_____	_____
_____	_____
_____	_____
_____	_____
_____	_____
_____	_____
_____	_____
_____	_____
_____	_____
_____	_____

Note: _____

_____

_____

_____

Recipe Name: _____

Prep Time: _____ *Cook Time:* _____ *Serves:* _____

Ingredients   ## Directions

_____   _____
_____   _____
_____   _____
_____   _____
_____   _____
_____   _____
_____   _____
_____   _____
_____   _____
_____   _____
_____   _____
_____   _____
_____   _____
_____   _____
_____   _____
_____   _____

Note: _____

_____
_____
_____

Page no.

Recipe Name: _____

Prep Time: _____ *Cook Time*: _____ *Serves*: _____

Ingredients   ## Directions

Ingredients	Directions
_____	_____
_____	_____
_____	_____
_____	_____
_____	_____
_____	_____
_____	_____
_____	_____
_____	_____
_____	_____
_____	_____
_____	_____
_____	_____
_____	_____
_____	

Note: _____

_____

_____

_____

Page no.

Recipe Name: _____

Prep Time: _____ *Cook Time:* _____ *Serves:* _____

Ingredients

_____

_____

_____

_____

_____

_____

_____

_____

_____

_____

_____

_____

_____

_____

_____

_____

Directions

_____

_____

_____

_____

_____

_____

_____

_____

_____

_____

_____

_____

_____

_____

_____

_____

Note: _____

_____

_____

_____

Page no.

Recipe Name: _____

Prep Time: _____ *Cook Time:* _____ *Serves:* _____

Ingredients

Directions

Note: _____

_____

_____

_____

Page no.

Recipe Name: _____

Prep Time: _____ *Cook Time:* _____ *Serves:* _____

Ingredients　　　　　　　　Directions

_____　　_____

_____　　_____

_____　　_____

_____　　_____

_____　　_____

_____　　_____

_____　　_____

_____　　_____

_____　　_____

_____　　_____

_____　　_____

_____　　_____

_____　　_____

_____　　_____

_____　　_____

Note: _____

_____

_____

_____

Recipe Name: _____

Prep Time: _____ *Cook Time:* _____ *Serves:* _____

Ingredients	**Directions**
_____	_____
_____	_____
_____	_____
_____	_____
_____	_____
_____	_____
_____	_____
_____	_____
_____	_____
_____	_____
_____	_____
_____	_____
_____	_____

Note: _____

_____

_____

_____

Page no.

Recipe Name: _____

Prep Time: _____ *Cook Time:* _____ *Serves:* _____

Ingredients   ## Directions

_____   _____

_____   _____

_____   _____

_____   _____

_____   _____

_____   _____

_____   _____

_____   _____

_____   _____

_____   _____

_____   _____

_____   _____

_____   _____

_____   _____

_____   _____

Note: _____

_____

_____

_____

Page no.

Recipe Name: _____

Prep Time: _____ *Cook Time:* _____ *Serves:* _____

Ingredients   ## Directions

_____   _____
_____   _____
_____   _____
_____   _____
_____   _____
_____   _____
_____   _____
_____   _____
_____   _____
_____   _____
_____   _____
_____   _____
_____   _____
_____   _____
_____   _____

Note: _____

_____

_____

_____

Page no.

Recipe Name: _____

Prep Time: _____ *Cook Time:* _____ *Serves:* _____

Ingredients   ## Directions

_____   _____

_____   _____

_____   _____

_____   _____

_____   _____

_____   _____

_____   _____

_____   _____

_____   _____

_____   _____

_____   _____

_____   _____

_____   _____

_____   _____

_____   _____

Note: _____

_____

_____

_____

Page no.

Recipe Name: _____

Prep Time: _____ *Cook Time:* _____ *Serves:* _____

Ingredients   ## *Directions*

_____ | _____

_____ | _____

_____ | _____

_____ | _____

_____ | _____

_____ | _____

_____ | _____

_____ | _____

_____ | _____

_____ | _____

_____ | _____

_____ | _____

_____ | _____

_____ | _____

Note: _____

_____

_____

_____

Page no.

Recipe Name: _____

Prep Time: _____ *Cook Time:* _____ *Serves:* _____

Ingredients   ## *Directions*

_____   _____
_____   _____
_____   _____
_____   _____
_____   _____
_____   _____
_____   _____
_____   _____
_____   _____
_____   _____
_____   _____
_____   _____
_____   _____

Note: _____

_____

_____

_____

Page no.

Recipe Name: _____

Prep Time: _____ *Cook Time:* _____ *Serves:* _____

Ingredients   ## *Directions*

_____   _____
_____   _____
_____   _____
_____   _____
_____   _____
_____   _____
_____   _____
_____   _____
_____   _____
_____   _____
_____   _____
_____   _____
_____   _____
_____   _____
_____   _____
_____   _____

Note: _____

_____
_____
_____

Page no.

Recipe Name: _____

Prep Time: _____ *Cook Time:* _____ *Serves:* _____

Ingredients	Directions

Note: _____

_____

_____

_____

Page no.

Recipe Name: _____

Prep Time: _____ *Cook Time:* _____ *Serves:* _____

Ingredients	*Directions*
_____	_____
_____	_____
_____	_____
_____	_____
_____	_____
_____	_____
_____	_____
_____	_____
_____	_____
_____	_____
_____	_____
_____	_____
_____	_____
_____	_____

Note: _____

_____

_____

_____

Page no.

Recipe Name: _____

Prep Time: _____ *Cook Time:* _____ *Serves:* _____

Ingredients

Directions

_____

_____

_____

_____

_____

_____

_____

_____

_____

_____

_____

_____

_____

Note: _____

_____

_____

_____

Recipe Name*:* _____

Prep Time: _____ *Cook Time:* _____ *Serves:* _____

Ingredients   *Directions*

_____ | _____

_____ | _____

_____ | _____

_____ | _____

_____ | _____

_____ | _____

_____ | _____

_____ | _____

_____ | _____

_____ | _____

_____ | _____

_____ | _____

_____ | _____

_____ | _____

Note: _____

_____

_____

_____

Recipe Name: _____

Prep Time: _____ *Cook Time:* _____ *Serves:* _____

Ingredients   ## Directions

_____   _____
_____   _____
_____   _____
_____   _____
_____   _____
_____   _____
_____   _____
_____   _____
_____   _____
_____   _____
_____   _____
_____   _____
_____   _____
_____   _____
_____   _____

Note: _____

_____

_____

_____

Page no.

Recipe Name: _____

Prep Time: _____ *Cook Time:* _____ *Serves:* _____

Ingredients   ## *Directions*

_____   _____
_____   _____
_____   _____
_____   _____
_____   _____
_____   _____
_____   _____
_____   _____
_____   _____
_____   _____
_____   _____
_____   _____
_____   _____
_____   _____
_____   _____

Note: _____

_____

_____

_____

Page no.

Recipe Name: _____

Prep Time: _____ *Cook Time:* _____ *Serves:* _____

Ingredients   ## Directions

_____   _____
_____   _____
_____   _____
_____   _____
_____   _____
_____   _____
_____   _____
_____   _____
_____   _____
_____   _____
_____   _____
_____   _____
_____   _____
_____   _____

Note: _____

_____

_____

_____

Page no.

Recipe Name: _____

Prep Time: _____ *Cook Time:* _____ *Serves:* _____

Ingredients   ## Directions

_____   _____
_____   _____
_____   _____
_____   _____
_____   _____
_____   _____
_____   _____
_____   _____
_____   _____
_____   _____
_____   _____
_____   _____
_____   _____
_____   _____
_____   _____

Note: _____

_____

_____

_____

Page no.

Recipe Name: _____

Prep Time: _____ *Cook Time:* _____ *Serves:* _____

Ingredients   ## Directions

_____   _____
_____   _____
_____   _____
_____   _____
_____   _____
_____   _____
_____   _____
_____   _____
_____   _____
_____   _____
_____   _____
_____   _____
_____   _____
_____   _____
_____   _____
_____   _____

Note: _____

_____

_____

_____

Page no.

Recipe Name: _____

Prep Time: _____ *Cook Time:* _____ *Serves:* _____

Ingredients   ## *Directions*

_____   _____
_____   _____
_____   _____
_____   _____
_____   _____
_____   _____
_____   _____
_____   _____
_____   _____
_____   _____
_____   _____
_____   _____
_____   _____
_____   _____

Note: _____
_____
_____
_____

Page no.

Recipe Name: _____

Prep Time: _____ *Cook Time:* _____ *Serves:* _____

Ingredients　　　　　　　　　*Directions*

_____　　_____

_____　　_____

_____　　_____

_____　　_____

_____　　_____

_____　　_____

_____　　_____

_____　　_____

_____　　_____

_____　　_____

_____　　_____

_____　　_____

_____　　_____

_____　　_____

_____　　_____

_____　　_____

Note: _____

_____

_____

_____

Page no.

Recipe Name: _____

Prep Time: _____ *Cook Time:* _____ *Serves:* _____

Ingredients	**Directions**
_____	_____
_____	_____
_____	_____
_____	_____
_____	_____
_____	_____
_____	_____
_____	_____
_____	_____
_____	_____
_____	_____
_____	_____
_____	_____
_____	_____
_____	_____

Note: _____

_____

_____

_____

Recipe Name: _____

Prep Time: _____ *Cook Time:* _____ *Serves:* _____

Ingredients   ## Directions

_____   _____
_____   _____
_____   _____
_____   _____
_____   _____
_____   _____
_____   _____
_____   _____
_____   _____
_____   _____
_____   _____
_____   _____
_____   _____
_____   _____
_____   _____

Note: _____

_____

_____

_____

Page no.

Recipe Name: _____

Prep Time: _____ *Cook Time:* _____ *Serves:* _____

Ingredients   ## *Directions*

_____ | _____

_____ | _____

_____ | _____

_____ | _____

_____ | _____

_____ | _____

_____ | _____

_____ | _____

_____ | _____

_____ | _____

_____ | _____

_____ | _____

_____ | _____

Note: _____

_____

_____

_____

Page no.

Recipe Name: _____

Prep Time: _____ *Cook Time:* _____ *Serves:* _____

Ingredients	Directions
_____	_____
_____	_____
_____	_____
_____	_____
_____	_____
_____	_____
_____	_____
_____	_____
_____	_____
_____	_____
_____	_____
_____	_____
_____	_____
_____	_____
_____	_____

Note: _____

_____

_____

_____

Page no.

Recipe Name: _____

Prep Time: _____ *Cook Time:* _____ *Serves:* _____

Ingredients   ## Directions

_____   _____
_____   _____
_____   _____
_____   _____
_____   _____
_____   _____
_____   _____
_____   _____
_____   _____
_____   _____
_____   _____
_____   _____
_____   _____
_____   _____
_____   _____

Note: _____

_____

_____

_____

Page no.

Recipe Name*: _____*

Prep Time: _____Cook Time: _____ Serves: _____

Ingredients   ## *Directions*

_____   _____
_____   _____
_____   _____
_____   _____
_____   _____
_____   _____
_____   _____
_____   _____
_____   _____
_____   _____
_____   _____
_____   _____
_____   _____
_____   _____
_____   _____

Note: _____

_____

_____

_____

Recipe Name: _____

Prep Time: _____ *Cook Time:* _____ *Serves:* _____

Ingredients   ## Directions

_____ | _____
_____ | _____
_____ | _____
_____ | _____
_____ | _____
_____ | _____
_____ | _____
_____ | _____
_____ | _____
_____ | _____
_____ | _____
_____ | _____
_____ | _____
_____ | _____

Note: _____

_____

_____

_____

Page no.

Recipe Name: _____

Prep Time: _____ *Cook Time:* _____ *Serves:* _____

Ingredients

Directions

_____   _____
_____   _____
_____   _____
_____   _____
_____   _____
_____   _____
_____   _____
_____   _____
_____   _____
_____   _____
_____   _____
_____   _____
_____   _____
_____   _____

Note: _____

_____

_____

_____

Recipe Name: _____

Prep Time: _____ *Cook Time:* _____ *Serves:* _____

Ingredients   ## Directions

_____ | _____
_____ | _____
_____ | _____
_____ | _____
_____ | _____
_____ | _____
_____ | _____
_____ | _____
_____ | _____
_____ | _____
_____ | _____
_____ | _____
_____ | _____
_____ | _____

Note: _____

_____

_____

_____

Page no.

Recipe Name: _____

Prep Time: _____ *Cook Time:* _____ *Serves:* _____

Ingredients   ## Directions

_____   _____

_____   _____

_____   _____

_____   _____

_____   _____

_____   _____

_____   _____

_____   _____

_____   _____

_____   _____

_____   _____

_____   _____

_____   _____

_____   _____

Note: _____

_____

_____

_____

| Page no. |

Recipe Name: _____

Prep Time: _____ *Cook Time:* _____ *Serves:* _____

Ingredients   ## *Directions*

_____ | _____

_____ | _____

_____ | _____

_____ | _____

_____ | _____

_____ | _____

_____ | _____

_____ | _____

_____ | _____

_____ | _____

_____ | _____

_____ | _____

_____ | _____

Note: _____

_____

_____

_____

Page no.

Recipe Name: _____

Prep Time: _____ *Cook Time:* _____ *Serves:* _____

Ingredients   ### Directions

_____   _____
_____   _____
_____   _____
_____   _____
_____   _____
_____   _____
_____   _____
_____   _____
_____   _____
_____   _____
_____   _____
_____   _____
_____   _____
_____   _____
_____   _____

Note: _____
_____
_____
_____

Page no.

Recipe Name: _____

Prep Time: _____ *Cook Time:* _____ *Serves:* _____

Ingredients	**Directions**
_____	_____
_____	_____
_____	_____
_____	_____
_____	_____
_____	_____
_____	_____
_____	_____
_____	_____
_____	_____
_____	_____
_____	_____
_____	_____
_____	_____
_____	_____

Note: _____

_____

_____

_____

Page no.

Recipe Name*: _____*

Prep Time: _____Cook Time: _____ Serves: _____

Ingredients   ## Directions

——————————   ——————————

——————————   ——————————

——————————   ——————————

——————————   ——————————

——————————   ——————————

——————————   ——————————

——————————   ——————————

——————————   ——————————

——————————   ——————————

——————————   ——————————

——————————   ——————————

——————————   ——————————

——————————   ——————————

——————————   ——————————

——————————   ——————————

Note: _____

_____

_____

_____

Page no.

Recipe Name: _____

Prep Time: _____ *Cook Time:* _____ *Serves:* _____

Ingredients   ## *Directions*

_____   _____
_____   _____
_____   _____
_____   _____
_____   _____
_____   _____
_____   _____
_____   _____
_____   _____
_____   _____
_____   _____
_____   _____
_____   _____
_____   _____

Note: _____

_____

_____

_____

Page no.

Recipe Name: _____

Prep Time: _____ *Cook Time:* _____ *Serves:* _____

Ingredients   ## Directions

Ingredients	Directions
_____	_____
_____	_____
_____	_____
_____	_____
_____	_____
_____	_____
_____	_____
_____	_____
_____	_____
_____	_____
_____	_____
_____	_____
_____	_____
_____	_____
_____	_____

Note: _____

_____

_____

_____

Page no.

Recipe Name*: _____*

Prep Time: _____Cook Time: _____ Serves: _____

Ingredients ## *Directions*

_____ _____

_____ _____

_____ _____

_____ _____

_____ _____

_____ _____

_____ _____

_____ _____

_____ _____

_____ _____

_____ _____

_____ _____

_____ _____

_____ _____

_____ _____

_____ _____

_____ _____

Note: _____

_____

_____

_____

Page no.

Recipe Name: _____

Prep Time: _____ *Cook Time:* _____ *Serves:* _____

Ingredients

Directions

_____
_____
_____
_____
_____
_____
_____
_____
_____
_____
_____
_____
_____
_____

Note: _____

_____

_____

_____

Page no.

Recipe Name: _____

Prep Time: _____ *Cook Time:* _____ *Serves:* _____

Ingredients   ## Directions

_____   _____
_____   _____
_____   _____
_____   _____
_____   _____
_____   _____
_____   _____
_____   _____
_____   _____
_____   _____
_____   _____
_____   _____
_____   _____
_____   _____

Note: _____
_____
_____
_____

Page no.

Recipe Name: _____

Prep Time: _____ *Cook Time:* _____ *Serves:* _____

Ingredients   ## Directions

_____   _____
_____   _____
_____   _____
_____   _____
_____   _____
_____   _____
_____   _____
_____   _____
_____   _____
_____   _____
_____   _____
_____   _____
_____   _____
_____   _____
_____   _____

Note: _____
_____
_____
_____

Page no.

***Recipe Name**:* _____

Prep Time: _____ *Cook Time:* _____ *Serves:* _____

Ingredients   ## *Directions*

_____   _____
_____   _____
_____   _____
_____   _____
_____   _____
_____   _____
_____   _____
_____   _____
_____   _____
_____   _____
_____   _____
_____   _____
_____   _____
_____   _____
_____   _____

Note: _____

_____

_____

_____

Page no.

Made in the USA
Las Vegas, NV
29 October 2021